POEMS FOR WINTER

Selected by
Robert Hull

Illustrated by
Annabel Spenceley

STECK-VAUGHN
L I B R A R Y
A Division of Steck-Vaughn Company

Austin, Texas

Seasonal Poetry

Poems for Autumn
Poems for Spring
Poems for Summer
Poems for Winter

Series Editor: Catherine Ellis
Designer: Ross George

Library of Congress Cataloging in Publication Data
Poems for winter / selected by Robert Hull : illustrated by Annabel
Spenceley
  p. cm. — (Seasonal poetry)
  Includes index.
  Summary: An anthology of poems reflecting winter by such authors
as Robert Frost, Carl Sandburg and A. A. Milne.
  ISBN 0-8114-7801-7
  1. Winter — Juvenile poetry. 2. Children's poetry. 3. Poetry —
Collections. 4. English poetry — Translations from foreign
languages. [1. Winter — Poetry. 2. Poetry — Collections.]
I. Hull, Robert. II. Spenceley, Annabel. ill. III. Series.
PN6109.97.P637 1991
808.81'933 – dc20   90-20589
                                                             CIP AC

Picture Acknowledgments
The publishers would like to thank the
following for allowing their illustrations to be
reproduced in this book: Bruce Coleman
(Fritz Prenzel) 13, (Hans Reinhard) 16, (Hans
Reinhard) 31, (Fritz Prenzel) 35; GeoScience
Features 15; Frank Lane Picture Agency (M.
J. Thomas) 26, (R. P. Lawrence) 39, (M.
Nimmo) 40; Topham Picture Library *Cover*,
8, 19, (Parkhouse) 43; Zefa (Fritz Bergman)
5, (S. Roessler) 7, (K Parker) 10, 23, (Herman
Jiri) 25, 29, (Bramaz) 32, (Orion Press) 36, 44.

Acknowledgments
For permission to reprint copyright material
the publishers gratefully acknowledge the
following: Faber & Faber Ltd for "Snowman
Sniffles" from *Snowman Sniffles* by N. M.
Bodecker; the Estate of Robert Frost, E.
Connery Lathem and Jonathan Cape Ltd for
"Looking for a Sunset Bird" and "Dust of
Snow" from *The Poetry of Robert Frost* edited
by Edward Connery Lathem; the author and
the Bodley Head for "I Have Six Arms" from
Speaking Crust by John Fuller; A. D. Peters
and Don Congdon Associates for "The
Father's Song" from *Book of the Eskimos* by
Peter Freuchen; J. M. Dent for N. M.
Bodecker's "When All the World is Full of
Snow"; Julie O'Callaghan for "A Blizzard on
Judson Avenue"; Rupert M. Loydell for
"Snow"; Irene Rawnsley for "Winter
Waking", "Who Came?", "Every Year"; John
Foster for "Gran"; Paul Coltman for "Owls";
Harcourt Brace Jovanovich for excerpt from
"The Prairie" by Carl Sandburg, from
Cornhuskers; Penguin Books USA for
"Happiness" and "Furry Bear" by A. A.
Milne; "Furry Bear" from *Now We are Six* by A. A.
Milne, copyright under the Berne
Convention, reproduced by permission of
Curtis Brown, London; "When All the World
is Full of Snow" and "Snowman Sniffles"
reprinted with permission of Margaret K.
McElderry Books, copyright © 1983 by N. M.
Bodecker, Cadbury for "Winter" by Ernest
Ogbonnaya from *Cadbury's Fifth Book of
Children's Poetry*.

While every effort has been made to secure
permission, in some cases it has proved
impossible to trace the copyright holders.
The publishers apologize for this apparent
negligence.

Typeset by Nicola Taylor, Wayland
Printed in Italy by G. Canale & C.S.p.A.
Bound in the United States.

1 2 3 4 5 Ca 95 94 93 92 91

Contents

Introduction

How many winters can you remember when it snowed? Two or three? Four? Even if you remember it being mainly cold and wet, it always seems to be snowing in poems about winter. Perhaps it's because that's how winter should be, and how you'd like it to be. Perhaps it's how poets remember it. Poets like snow in the same way that children do, because you can do nice things with it – throw it at teachers who don't mind, put it down your best friend's neck. Poets like making snowmen and throwing snowballs. They like watching car wheels spin. They like watching children frolicking in the snow. They like the way snow upsets things. You can't get to school, cars get stuck, buses don't come. Like you, they enjoy the way snow alters everything, so for a day or two life gets thoroughly messed up and put off its stride and has to stop for a think.

But there's another side to winter. Many living creatures are threatened by the cold coming. The cold hurts insects, birds, and old people. Poets notice these things, too.

If you can do what poets do, perhaps you can be a poet. Go out and look at things, and then write about what you see.

5

Happiness

John had
Great Big
Waterproof
Boots on;
John had a
Great Big
Waterproof
Hat;
John had a
Great Big
Waterproof
Mackintosh –
And that
(Said John)
    Is
    That.

A. A. MILNE

Every Year

Winter walks in
every year;
blows your brains
from ear to ear,

Slaps your face
with icy drops,
turns your toes
to organ stops.

IRENE RAWNSLEY

Snow

The sky
has talcum-powdered
between the toes
of the world.

RUPERT M. LOYDELL

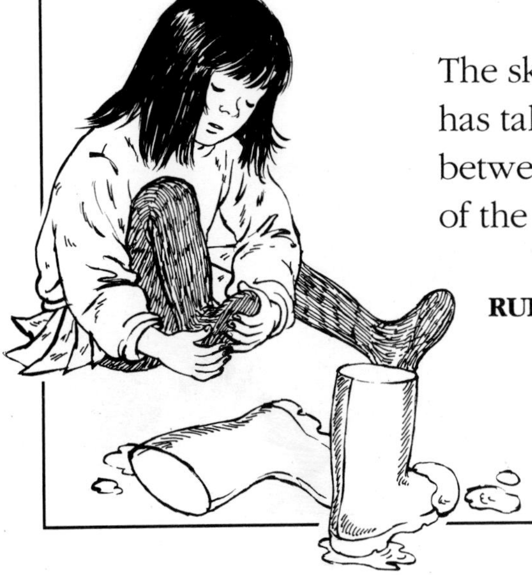

9

Gran

In winter Gran got chilblains.
Calling to see her
On the way home from school
I'd catch her with her skirt
Up round her knees,
Her feet immersed
In a white enamel bowl
Full of a steaming yellow liquid –
A mustard bath.

Gran's gone now.
Instead of mustard powder,
We buy our mustard in pots
From the supermarket.
When I had chilblains,
The doctor gave me a prescription
For an ointment from the chemist.
As I rubbed it on,
I thought of Gran,
The white enamel bowl,
The yellow liquid,
Her feet swollen and chapped,
Her mittened hands.

JOHN FOSTER

chilblains – swelling or sores from exposure to the cold.

Dust of Snow

The way a crow
Shook down on me
The dust of snow
From a hemlock tree

Has given my heart
A change of mood
And saved some part
Of a day I had rued.

ROBERT FROST

Who Came?

Footprints in the snow.
Who was it came
in the night,
taking the short cut?

IRENE RAWNSLEY

Winter Waking

Can this be day?
It looks like night,
So thin and sulky
is the light.

A lonely sweeper
in the street
disturbs the dust
of last night's feet

And curtains open
splinter wide
give little sign
of life inside.

A stubborn car
with cough and wheeze
resents the turning
of the keys

While clockwork birds
sing "tin, tin, tin,"
to woo the weary
morning in;

And singing, singing
in my head,
How safe it was,
how warm,
in bed.

IRENE RAWNSLEY

On a Night of Snow

Cat, if you go outdoors, you must walk in the snow.
You will come back with little white shoes on your feet,
little white shoes of snow that have heels of sleet.
Stay by the fire, my Cat. Lie still, do not go.
See how the flames are leaping and hissing low,
I will bring you a saucer of milk like a marguerite,
so white and so smooth, so spherical and so sweet –
stay with me, Cat. Outdoors the wild winds blow.

Outdoors the wild winds blow, Mistress, and dark is the night,
strange voices cry in the trees, intoning strange lore,
and more than cats move, lit by our eyes' green light,
on silent feet where the meadow grasses hang hoar –
Mistress, there are portents abroad of magic and might,
and things that are yet to be done. Open the door!

ELIZABETH COATSWORTH

marguerite – a daisy.

hoar – frosted.

17

Owls

Who? Close as darkness.
Who? Whose cold voices
trembling in the trees?

The owls are calling.
Ice in their voices.
Moon in their glittering eyes.

Cocooned in dreams
my sleep is troubled
by the owls' calling

till the black throat
of the early cock splits
night for the furious sun

to spring up singing.

PAUL COLTMAN

The Father's Song

Great snowslide,
Stay away from my igloo,
I have my four children and my wife;
They can never enrich you.

Strong snowslide,
Roll past my weak house.
There sleep my dear ones in the world.
Snowslide, let their night be calm.

Sinister snowslide,
I just built an igloo here, sheltered from the wind.
It is my fault if it is put wrong.
Snowslide, hear me from your mountain.

Greedy snowslide,
There is enough to smash and smother.
Fall down over the ice,
Bury stones and cliffs and rocks.

Greedy snowslide, I own so little in the world.
Keep away from our igloo, stop not our travels.
Nothing will you gain by our horror and death,
Mighty snowslide, mighty snowslide.

Little snowslide,
Four children and my wife are my whole world, all I own,
All I can lose, nothing can you gain.
Snowslide, save my house, stay on your summit.

ANONYMOUS (Translated from the Inuit by Peter Freuchen)

A Blizzard on Judson Avenue

A family in eskimo coats waddles past on snowshoes
and a black poodle wearing a tartan ensemble
tiptoes by with red boots.
Two girls in striped hats
struggle through the powdery drifts
with their tongues out, trying to catch a snowflake.
A young executive, with a Christmas tree trunk
at his neck, groans and leaves a mark
like the dragging tail of a peacock.
I open the crystal window and listen for life.
There is no sound anywhere
except the scraping of a sled
piled with grocery bags
gliding down the middle of the street.
By morning, wind and snow
will have repaired the damage.

JULIE O'CALLAGHAN

23

Limited Crossing Wisconsin

A headlight searches a snowstorm.
A funnel of white light shoots from over the pilot of the
   Pioneer Limited crossing Wisconsin.

In the morning hours, in the dawn,
The sun puts out the stars of the sky
And the headlight of the Limited train.

The fireman waves his hand to a country school
   teacher on a bobsled.
A boy, yellow hair, red scarf and mittens, on the
   bobsled, in his lunch box a pork chop sandwich and a
      V of gooseberry pie.

The horses fathom a snow to their knees.
Snow hats are on the rolling prairie hills.
The Mississippi bluffs wear snow hats.

CARL SANDBURG

When All the World Is Full of Snow

I never know
just where to go,
when all the world
is full of snow.

I do not want
to make a track,
not even
to the shed and back.

I only want
to watch and wait,
while snow moths settle
on the gate,

and swarming frost flakes
fill the trees
with billions
of albino bees.

I only want
myself to be
as silent as
a winter tree,

to hear the swirling
stillness grow,
when all the world
is full of snow.

N. M. BODECKER

Furry Bear

If I were a bear
   And a big bear too,
I shouldn't much care
   If it froze or snew;
I shouldn't much mind
   If it snowed or friz –
I'd be all fur-lined
   With a coat like his!

For I'd have fur boots and a brown fur wrap,
And brown fur knickers and a big fur cap.
I'd have a fur muffle-ruff to cover my jaws,
And brown fur mittens on my big brown paws.
With a big brown furry-down up to my head,
I'd sleep all the winter in a big fur bed.

A. A. MILNE

That Cat

The cat that comes to my window sill
When the moon looks cold and the night is still –
He comes in a frenzied state alone
With a tail that stands like a pine tree cone,
And says: "I have finished my evening lark,
And I think I can hear a hound dog bark.
My whiskers are froze and stuck to my chin.
I do wish you'd git up and let me in."
   That cat gits in.

But if in the solitude of the night
He doesn't appear to be feeling right,
And rises and stretches and seeks the floor,
And some remote corner he would explore,
And doesn't feel satisfied just because
There's no good spot for to sharpen his claws,
And meows and canters uneasy about
Beyond the least shadow of any doubt
   That cat gits out.

BEN KING

lark – escapade or adventure.

Riddle

I have six arms
And swallow farms.

Millions can
Become a man.

I cannot fly
Backwards. I die

When life burgeons.
My tearful sons

Destroy my shape,
My perfect shape.

JOHN FULLER

Looking for a Sunset Bird in Winter

The west was getting out of gold,
The breath of air had died of cold,
When shoeing home across the white,
I thought I saw a bird alight.

In summer when I passed the place
I had to stop and lift my face;
A bird with an angelic gift
Was singing in it sweet and swift.

No bird was singing in it now.
A single leaf was on a bough,
And that was all there was to see
In going twice around the tree.

From my advantage on a hill
I judged that such a crystal chill
Was only adding frost to snow
As gilt to gold that wouldn't show.

A brush had left a crooked stroke
Of what was either cloud or smoke
From north to south across the blue;
A piercing little star was through.

ROBERT FROST

alight – land.

Winter Haiku

A bitter morning:
    sparrows sitting together
      without any necks.

J. W. HACKETT

Ice in a Stream

Across thousands of mountains no birds fly,
Across thousands of paths there are no footprints.
On a lonely boat lies an old fisherman
Fishing solitarily in the ice of a frozen stream.

LIU TSUNG-YUAN

Sheep in Winter

The sheep get up and make their many tracks
And bear a load of snow upon their backs,
And gnaw the frozen turnip to the ground
With sharp quick bite, and then go noising round
The boy that pecks the turnips all the day
And knocks his hands to keep the cold away
And laps his legs in straw to keep them warm
And hides behind the hedges from the storm.
The sheep, as tame as dogs, go where he goes
And try to shake their fleeces from the snows,
Then leave their frozen meal and wander round
The stubble stack that stands beside the ground,
And lie all night and face the drizzling storm
And shun the hovel where they might be warm.

JOHN CLARE

39

Small, smaller

I thought that I knew all there was to know
Of being small, until I saw once, black against the snow,
A shrew, trapped in my footprint, jump and fall
And jump again and fall, the hole too deep, the walls too tall.

RUSSELL HOBAN

Winter

It is cold today,
On the window this morning is a pattern.
There's a puddle of glass in the street.
Your cheeks are red as if they are on fire.
I shall warm my hands on your red cheeks.

ERNEST OGBONNAYA (Age 7)

The Tough Guy of London

Seen from within a heated room,
On a sunny February afternoon,
London looks like
Any other summer's day.

Step out in only
Your shirt and trousers
And, even with a black belt in karate,
An invisible tough guy
With blimey cold hands and feet,
Punches you
Smack on the nose
Straight back in.

KOJO GYINAYE KYEI

blimey – very.

Snowman Sniffles

At winter's end
a snowman grows
a snowdrop
on his carrot nose,

a little, sad,
late-season sniff
dried by the spring
wind's handkerchief.

But day and night
the sniffles drop
like flower buds
– they never stop,

until you wake
and find one day
the cold, old man
has run away,

and winter's winds
that blow and pass
left drifts of snowdrops
in the grass,

reminding us:
where such things grow
a snowman sniffled
not long ago.

N. M. BODECKER

Biographies

N. M. Bodecker was born in Denmark, and now lives in the U.S. He spent his early life painting and drawing, then started to write at about twenty. He has three sons and lives in New Hampshire in an old haunted house.

John Clare (1793–1864) was born in Helpston, Northamptonshire, England, the son of a farm laborer. He taught himself, becoming a successful writer even while working as a laborer. He had a sad life. He became ill, and spent the last twenty-three years of his life in an asylum, dying there in 1864.

Elizabeth Coatsworth was born in Buffalo, New York, in 1893. She traveled a great deal even as a child. In later life she wrote poems for adults and children, including *The Cat Who Went to Heaven*.

Paul Coltman lives in Sussex, England. He has published collections of poems for adults, and books for children – the well-known *Tog the Ribber*, and *Witch Watch* (illustrated by his daughter, Gillian McClure).

John Foster has been a teacher and a school headteacher. As well as writing poetry for children he has compiled several anthologies, written books about teaching, and worked on radio and television.

Robert Frost (1874–1963) is one of the most famous American poets of this century. He was born in California, and later lived on a farm in New Hampshire. Although he did not write especially for children, many of his poems are children's favorites.

John Fuller was born in Kent, England, in 1937. He is married with three daughters. He has written several books for children, including a pantomime opera, *The Spider Monkey Uncle King*.

Russell Hoban is a very well-known children's writer. He has written several picture-books, and a number of long stories such as *The Mouse and The Child*.

Rupert M. Loydell is a painter and publisher as well as a writer. He lives in Devon, England, where he founded Stride Publications. He has written several books, and his poems have appeared in many magazines and anthologies. His book of poems for children is called *The Fantasy Kid*.

A. A. Milne (1882–1956) wrote the famous Pooh stories for his son Christopher Robin, and his two books of poems for children – *When We Were Very Young* and *Now We Are Six* – are among the most popular children's poems ever written.

Julie O'Callaghan was born in Chicago in 1954, and now lives in Dublin. She has written and edited several books, including *Taking My Pen for a Walk*, which was published in 1988.

Ernest Ogbonnaya was only seven years old when he wrote the poem in this book. It was "highly commended" by the judges of the 5th Cadbury's Poetry Competition. He was at Turnham Junior School, Brockley, England; we think he must be ten now.

Irene Rawnsley lives in Settle, Yorkshire, England. In 1988 she published a collection of poems for children called *Ask a Silly Question*. A second book, called *Dog's Dinner*, was published in 1990.

Carl Sandburg (1878–1967) was an American writer. He wrote many stories and poems for children. They are collected in a beautiful book called *The Sandburg Treasury*.

Liu Tsung-Yuan lived in China from AD 773 to 819. He was a famous calligrapher as well as a poet and civil servant.

Index of First Lines

First published in 1990 by
Wayland (Publishers) Ltd

© Copyright 1990 Wayland
(Publishers) Ltd